Stories of GREAT PEOPLE

Columbus's chart

Gerry Bailey and Karen Foster

**Illustrated by Leighton Noyes
and Karen Radford**

🌳 Crabtree Publishing Company
www.crabtreebooks.com

Mr. RUMMAGE has a stall piled high with interesting objects—and he has a great story to tell about each and every one of his treasures.

DIGBY PLATT is an antique collector. Every Saturday he picks up a bargain at Mr. Rummage's antique stall and loves listening to the story behind his new 'find'.

HANNAH PLATT is Digby's argumentative, older sister—and she doesn't believe a word that Mr. Rummage says!

Mrs. BILGE pushes her dustcart around the market, picking up litter. Trouble is, she's always throwing away the objects on Mr. Rummage's stall.

Mr. CLUMPMUGGER has an amazing collection of ancient maps, dusty books, and old newspapers in his rare prints stall.

J970.01
Bailey

Crabtree Publishing Company
www.crabtreebooks.com

Other books in the series

Cleopatra's coin

Leonardo's palette

Armstrong's moon rock

The Wright Brothers' glider

Shakespeare's quill

Marco Polo's silk purse

Mother Teresa's alms bowl

Sitting Bull's tomahawk

Martin Luther King, Jr.'s microphone

Credits

Cover image: Mary Evans Picture Library.
AKG Images: 28 bottom left
Ayuntamiento de Coruna, Spain/Bridgeman Art Library:
   24 top right
Bodleian Library, Oxford/Art Archive: 13 center left
British Library, London/HIP/Topham: 13 top right, 23 bottom
Mary Evans Picture Library: 20 bottom left, 20 top right,
   31 bottom right, 32 bottom
Fondation Thiers, Paris/Dagli Orti/Art Archive: 16 center left
Chris Hellier/Corbis: 12
Naval Museum Genoa/Dagli Orti/Art Archive: 10
New York Public Library/Art Archive: 19 bottom, 31 center right
Palazzo Pitti Florence/Dagli Orti /Art Archive: 23 center left
Photogenes: 24 bottom left
Picturepoint/Topham: 9, 13 bottom right, 15 top, 35 bottom right
Royal Geographical Society, London/Bridgeman Art Library:
   16 top right
World History Archive/Topfoto: 27 center left

Picture research: Diana Morris info@picture-research.co.uk

Library and Archives Canada Cataloguing in Publication

Bailey, Gerry
        Columbus's chart / Gerry Bailey and Karen Foster ;
illustrated
by Leighton Noyes and Karen Radford.

(Stories of great people)
Includes index.
ISBN 978-0-7787-3686-8 (bound).--ISBN 978-0-7787-3708-7 (pbk.)

        1. Columbus, Christopher, ca. 1451-1506--Juvenile fiction.
2. Explorers--Spain--Biography--Juvenile fiction. 3. Explorers--
America--Biography--Juvenile fiction. 4. America--Discovery and
exploration--Spanish--Juvenile fiction. I. Foster, Karen, 1959-
II. Noyes, Leighton III. Radford, Karen IV. Title. V. Series.

PZ7.B15Co 2008   j823'.92   C2007-907616-5

Library of Congress Cataloging-in-Publication Data

Bailey, Gerry.
  Columbus's chart / Gerry Bailey and Karen Foster ; illustrated by Leighton Noyes
and Karen Radford.
      p. cm. -- (Stories of great people)
  Includes index.
  ISBN-13: 978-0-7787-3686-8 (rlb)
  ISBN-10: 0-7787-3686-5 (rlb)
  ISBN-13: 978-0-7787-3708-7 (pb)
  ISBN-10: 0-7787-3708-X (pb)
  1. Columbus, Christopher--Travel--America--Juvenile literature. 2. America--
Description and travel--Juvenile literature. 3. Atlantic Ocean--Description and travel-
-Juvenile literature. 4. Columbus, Christopher--Juvenile literature. 5. Explorers--
America--Biography--Juvenile literature. 6. Explorers--Spain--Biography--Juvenile
literature. 7. America--Discovery and exploration--Spanish--Juvenile literature. I.
Foster, Karen. II. Noyes, Leighton, ill. III. Radford, Karen, ill. IV. Title.
  E118.B35 2008
  970.01'5--dc22
                                                2007051250

Crabtree Publishing Company

www.crabtreebooks.com   1-800-387-7650

Published in Canada
Crabtree Publishing
616 Welland Ave.
St. Catharines, Ontario
L2M 5V6

Published in the United States
Crabtree Publishing
PMB16A
350 Fifth Ave., Suite 3308
New York, NY 10118

Published by CRABTREE PUBLISHING COMPANY
Copyright © **2008** Diverta Ltd.

Columbus's Chart

Table of Contents

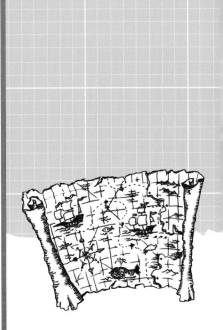

Knicknack Market comes to life	6
Columbus	9
Port of Genoa	10
Lisbon	13
Royal sponsors	15
Columbus's journeys	16
Three ships	19
Life aboard	20
At the helm	22
Land ahoy!	24
The Grand Fleet	27
A new continent	28
The high voyage	31
Homeward bound	32
The Americas	35
The truth and the legend	36
Glossary & Index	37

Every Saturday morning, Knicknack Market comes to life. The street vendors are there almost before the sun is up. And by the time you and I are out of bed, the stalls are built, the boxes are opened, and all the goods carefully laid out on display.

Objects are piled high. Some are laid out on velvet: precious necklaces and jeweled swords. Others stand upright at the back:

large, framed pictures of very important people, lamps made from tasseled satin and old-fashioned cash registers—the kind that jingle when the drawers are opened.

And then there are things that stay in their boxes all day, waiting for the right customer to come along: war medals laid out in straight lines, old stopwatches, and utensils in polished silver for all those special occasions.

But Mr. Rummage's stall is different. Mr. Rummage of Knicknack Market has a stall piled high with a disorderly jumble of things that no one could ever want.

Who wants to buy a stuffed mouse? Or a broken umbrella? Or a pair of false teeth?

Mr. Rummage has them all. And, as you can imagine, they don't cost a lot!

Rummage's
Antiques

Digby Platt hums cheerfully as he walks down the street toward Mr. Rummage's stall. Ten-year-old Digby is an antique collector of some standing—or at least he thinks so—and he's sure his friend Mr. Rummage will have found him another bargain today. Hannah, Digby's older sister, strides along beside him, equally sure that Mr. Rummage will tell another one of his tales, just to sell something to her brother.

As usual, Mr. Rummage's stall was a mess. There were piles of odds and ends lying all over the place.

"Hi, kids!" said Mr. Rummage from behind a stack of boxes. "Come on in. I could use your help. I've lost a very important chart."

"Maybe you've thrown it out with the garbage," said Hannah knowingly, as she saw Mrs. Bilge push her cart away from Mr. Rummage's stall and rumble off down the street. "Wait!" she yelled. "Mrs. Bilge, wait a minute."

"What now? Why folks can't leave a person alone to do a job, I don't know," grumbled Mrs. Bilge as she stopped and turned around. "And that place of Mr. Rummage's is a disaster..."

"Thanks," interrupted Hannah as she reached the cart, "Can I just...?" and she began searching the cart.

"What are you looking for young lady?" demanded the irritated Mrs. Bilge.

"Found it!" cried Hannah, holding up a thick, yellowed piece of paper that looked like old parchment.

"What do you want that junk for?" asked Mrs. Bilge, screwing up her nose.

"That's not junk," exclaimed Mr. Rummage. "That's a chart. But it's no ordinary one. This is Christopher Columbus's chart! Thanks Mrs. Bilge for being so, uh, tidy."

"My pleasure," snorted Mrs. Bilge, crossing her arms.

"And who, exactly, is Christopher Columbus?" asked Hannah suspiciously, as Digby's eyes lit up with excitement.

"Christopher Columbus was an explorer," said Mr. Rummage. "He was the man who discovered the Americas."

COLUMBUS'S COAT OF ARMS

In 1451 Christopher Columbus was born in the bustling seaport of Genoa in northern Italy. He was christened Christoforo Columbo, but most people know him by the English version of his name: Christopher Columbus.

When Christopher grew up, he became a sailor. His ambition was to explore the seas and find a quick route to Asia, or the Indies, as it was called then. He planned an **expedition** to get to these eastern lands by sailing west. Eventually, he sailed across the Atlantic Ocean as planned, but he didn't reach Asia—because the Americas got in the way.

Let's find out more...

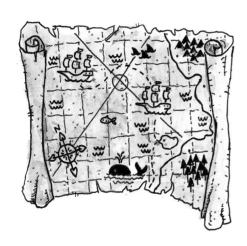

In the Middle Ages, Genoa was a busy port and an important center of trade in what is now Italy. By the time Christopher was born, it had become a wealthy city-state of merchants, bankers, and ship owners.

CHRISTOPHER WAS TAUGHT TO READ AND WRITE BY MONKS. THEY ALSO TAUGHT HIM ASTRONOMY AND GEOMETRY, SKILLS HE WOULD LATER NEED TO HELP HIM NAVIGATE ON HIS VOYAGES OF DISCOVERY.

Christopher's family

Christopher Columbus was born in a little house near the harbor. His father was called Domenico Colombo and his mother's name was Susanna Fontanarossa. Christopher's life was full of ups and downs right from the start. Sometimes his family were so poor they couldn't put food on the table. At other times, they ate well. It all depended on whether his father's merchant friends were in power in the city.

Ship's boy

In his teens, Columbus worked as a ship's boy and then as a sailor. He traveled to Greece, Spain, Portugal , and even Iceland, seeing and learning new things about the world as he went. His experiences would soon be very useful.

"The Americas are huge." said Digby. "That's right, the area includes the continents of North and South America. Continents are the largest areas of land on Earth," explained Mr. Rummage as he picked up a globe from a shelf behind him. "There are seven continents in the world."

"I know," said Hannah, looking pleased with herself, "they're called Asia, Africa, Antarctica, Europe, Australia, North America, and South America."

"Okay, but now can you tell us about Columbus," asked Digby, looking at Mr. Rummage eagerly.

"Sure! His story actually begins in Genoa, a city on the northwest coast of Italy," said Mr. Rummage, pointing to the place on the globe where the city was marked. "His father, Domenico, was a weaver and young Christopher used to help him at his work. He joined his father's wool business for a while, but he loved to escape to the busy harbor to see the merchants' ships coming in with silks and spices from the East. Like many young **Genoese** men, he dreamed of becoming a sailor."

"What did he look like? Don't you have a photo?" challenged Hannah.

"Columbus did grow up to be a tall, strong man," said Mr. Rummage with a twinkle in his eye, "but there weren't any cameras in the 1400s, so we only have a few statues and portraits to go by."

"By the time Christopher was 25, he was an experienced seaman. But he had his share of bad luck."

"What sort of bad luck? Was he ever **shipwrecked**?" asked Digby.

"As a matter of fact, he was. In 1476 he sailed with a fleet of Genoese merchant ships bound for England. But he didn't make it. The fleet was attacked by pirates off the Strait of Gibraltar and Christopher's ship was burned."

"How did he escape?" asked Digby.

"He survived by hanging on to a broken oar. After hours at sea, he finally made it to the Portuguese coast and crawled ashore. From there he made his way to the capital city, Lisbon."

A useful marriage

In 1479, Christopher married Dona Felipe Perestello, the daughter of a noble. Through his marriage, Columbus was able to meet important people and experienced sailors who gave him useful help and advice. Dona Felipe also gave him charts and documents belonging to her father, who'd been governor of the island of Madeira. They helped him learn more about Portuguese discoveries. Dona Felipe died shortly after giving birth to Diego, their son, in 1480.

Lisbon

Portugal was rich, and many Genoese moved there because it was the world's greatest seafaring nation. So Christopher decided to fulfill his dream of becoming a sea captain and settled in Lisbon. When not working as a mapmaker in his brother's workshop, Columbus spent the next few years traveling around the African coast. Soon, he knew the ocean as well as any **mariner** alive.

A visionary sailor

Columbus first took his "Enterprise of the Indies" plan to King John of Portugal. But the king was persuaded by his advisers that the trip would be too expensive. Besides, the king's mariners accused Columbus of being a dreamer who had got his facts wrong. They thought that only "worthless islands" existed in the western ocean.

IN COLUMBUS'S DAY, THE WORLD AS WE KNOW IT WAS LARGELY UNCHARTED.

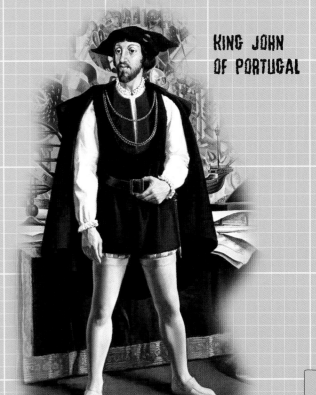

KING JOHN OF PORTUGAL

Around the globe

Lisbon was the westernmost city in Europe. No one really knew what lay beyond it. Christopher became convinced that he could reach Asia and the riches of the Indies by sailing west across the Atlantic Ocean. Other explorers thought they had to sail east to get to the Indies. Columbus was determined to prove them wrong.

13

"I bet the Portuguese kicked themselves later," grinned Hannah.

"You're probably right, because Christopher decided to take his plan to the King and Queen of Spain instead."

"And did they support him?"

"Not quite," said Mr. Rummage. "In fact, it took seven years to strike a deal."

"What!" exclaimed Hannah.

"Yes, seven years. Anyway, when Columbus and his son arrived in Spain, they met a friar called Juan Perez. This turned out to be a lucky meeting because Perez was the royal confessor. He introduced Columbus to the court of King Ferdinand and Queen Isabella."

"Did they agree with Christopher's plan?" asked Digby.

"They were interested, but the time wasn't right. Ferdinand and Isabella were too busy fighting against the Moors—Muslims who'd occupied Spain for hundreds of years—to pay much attention."

"And did they win the fight?"

"Yes, Digby, they did—and that changed things," said Mr. Rummage.

"The Spanish forces won the Battle of Granada and the Moors were kicked out of Spain. Now Ferdinand and Isabella could concentrate on Columbus."

"About time, too!" said Hannah.

When Columbus was summoned to the glittering court of King Ferdinand of Spain and his young wife Isabella, he had high hopes. He boldly told them of his elaborate plan to explore the far-off lands of China and Japan. But they weren't convinced by his ideas and sent him away.

ROYAL STANDARD

ROYAL COAT OF ARMS

It's a deal!

For seven long years Columbus tried to persuade them. In the end, he lost hope and left the Spanish court penniless and on a mule. But just as he was going out of the city gates, he was ordered to come back and do business. It was probably Queen Isabella, with her intelligence and education, who finally allowed Columbus the means to sail for the Indies. King Ferdinand was more interested in filling the empty **coffers** in his treasury after years of being at war.

Columbus's reward

But Columbus's journey wasn't going to be cheap. He demanded one-tenth of all the gold, spices, silks, and slaves Spain would receive from the new lands he visited. On top of this, he wanted to be made "Admiral of the Oceans" and be allowed to govern the lands he discovered. In return for their help, Columbus, who was a devout Catholic, promised he would represent the religion in the Indies and make sure that the people who lived there were converted to the Catholic faith.

Columbus's journeys

The first voyage

Columbus set out from Palos on August 3, 1492. His three ships headed south to the Canary Islands where they met the Canary current, which took them west. On October 12, a lookout spotted land. No one knows where they landed, but it might have been Watling Island or Semana Cay in the Bahamas.

The second voyage

Columbus made a second trip in September, 1493. On the second voyage, he had a Grand Fleet of 17 ships and 1300 men. He and his crew explored areas along the coast. Today, those lands are called Cuba, Jamaica, and Hispaniola.

The third voyage

On his third voyage, which took two years (1498-1500), Columbus explored a part of South America and even planted a Spanish flag on what is now called Venezuela.

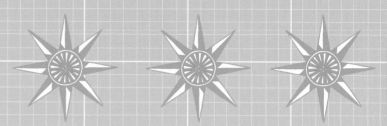

The fourth voyage

Columbus's fourth and last voyage was from 1502 to 1504. This time, he had only four ships and he sailed to Mexico, Honduras, and Panama.

"Ferdinand and Isabella were shrewd," said Mr. Rummage. "The town of Palos owed them some money, so they ordered the townspeople to provide Columbus with three fully-equipped ships. The first was called the Pinta. The second was called the Santa Clara, but was known as the Nina. And the third, a slightly larger ship, was called the Santa Maria."

"And this chart was the one Christopher used onboard the Santa Maria?" asked Digby hopefully.

"Of course," answered Mr. Rummage. "It's the one he drew when he went on his first voyage. And it is very valuable, too."

"I'd love to add this to my collection," said Digby, excitedly. "Imagine having the map that actually led to the discovery of the New World! I'll show it to all my friends."

"Huh!" said Hannah with a shake of her head. She hadn't believed a word that Mr. Rummage had said.

"I guess the voyage must have taken a long time," said Digby, ignoring his sister. "The Americas were so far away."

"Well," said Mr. Rummage, "the first crossing didn't take that long, considering what they were sailing in. But Columbus actually went on four voyages to the Americas. And even then he didn't find the Indies he was looking for."

"But he thought he had," said Hannah.

"Yes," continued Mr. Rummage, "but it never crossed his mind that he'd found a new continent. Or perhaps he just didn't want to know."

"In the days of Columbus, ships were made of wood, usually oak wood, and had three masts," explained Mr. Rummage. "They were called caravels. Somewhere I've got a small model of a wooden ship that I think is a caravel. I've kept it for you."

Digby gave him a broad smile as the storyteller walked over to a shelf piled high with junk and then came back with a small glass bottle. Inside the bottle was a tiny model ship. "Wow!" cried Digby as he peered into the bottle curiously.

"It's so small, I can hardly see a thing on it," said Hannah, shrugging her shoulders.

The crew

At first, Columbus had problems getting a crew together. Many sailors were afraid to journey into the unknown, and others had heard strange tales of monsters lurking under the waves far out at sea.

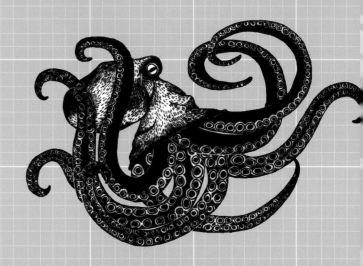

King Ferdinand and Queen Isabella offered to free any convict who wanted to sign up, but only four accepted. At last, Captain Pinzon managed to persuade local sailors from around Palos to come aboard. In the end about 90 men sailed with Columbus. They included a goldsmith, a surgeon, a physician, a secretary, a translator, a royal steward, a petty officer, and an accountan

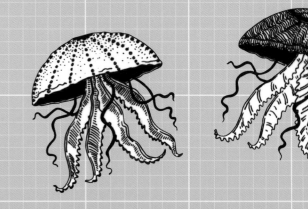

Three ships

The little fleet of three ships that sailed bravely out of Palos, flags flying, would seem like bath toys compared to the vessels of today. The Nina and the Pinta were small, light, and easy to turn in the wind—just right for exploring reefs, shallow bays, and river mouths. The Santa Maria, was shorter and rounder and sat very low in the water.

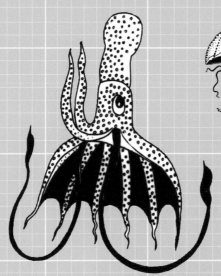

COLUMBUS WASN'T THAT IMPRESSED WITH HIS FLAGSHIP. HE THOUGHT IT LOOKED LIKE A TUB AND WOULD BE FAR TOO HEAVY AND UNWIELDY FOR THE TRIP. HE WAS RIGHT.

Life aboard

Life aboard one of Columbus's ships would have been very uncomfortable. The deck was usually awash with seawater and crowded with sailors, and the holds were packed with supplies and noisy, smelly livestock. Along with food and a repair kit, the ships also carried weapons, just in case they were attacked by pirates or unfriendly people when they found land.

A hard life

Out in the ocean, the sailors were at the mercy of the wind and waves. Whenever a storm broke, rain lashed the decks, wind roared through the **rigging**, and wild, foaming waves as high as the mast tossed the boat around on the water. If the ship rolled over, it could not right itself. And even if the fleet returned home safely, many of its crew would not. It wasn't easy being a sailor in Columbus's day!

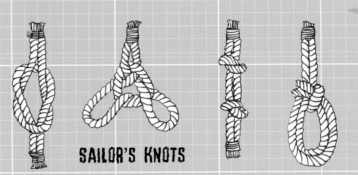

SAILOR'S KNOTS

COLUMBUS MEASURED THE SPEED OF HIS SHIP BY THROWING A PIECE OF DRIFTWOOD INTO THE WATER AT THE BOW AND SEEING HOW LONG IT TOOK TO GET TO THE STERN. IT WASN'T A VERY RELIABLE METHOD, BUT IT WAS THE BEST HE HAD AT THE TIME.

A day at sea

The crew worked four-hour shifts. The day began with prayers and hymns, and then duties, including repairing the sails and rigging, checking the cargo, manning the pumps and mopping the deck. They ate one hot meal a day, which was cooked over an open fire in a sandpit on deck. The day ended with more prayers. At night, sailors passed the time by swapping stories, singing songs, or just gazing at the stars.

Mariner's menu

A sailor's menu wasn't very appetizing: pickled fish or salted meat, maggoty bread, moldy cheese, stewed peas, and watered down wine—if you were lucky. The drinking water soon became green and slimy and the food rotted, causing disease and starvation on long voyages.

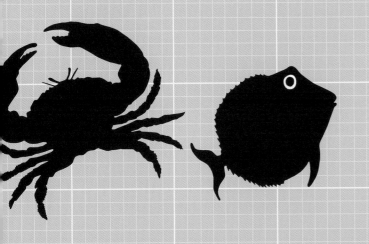

"There wasn't much room, even on large ships, in Columbus's day," said Mr. Rummage.

"Didn't the sailors have cabins?" asked Digby.

"No, Digby. Only the captain had private quarters. Imagine having nowhere to sleep except the open deck. Although you might have found a dry spot on the raised deck in the back or in a coil of rope, if you were lucky."

"What about food and water? Columbus must have carried supplies. What did everyone eat?" asked Digby.

"I bet they caught live fish and cooked them," said Hannah.

"They probably did, Hannah. Even though most voyages didn't last longer than two weeks, in those days most ships would carry a year's supply, just to be on the safe side," explained Mr. Rummage.

"So Columbus didn't really have much of an idea where he was going," suggested Digby.

"Well, he didn't have accurate maps, so he didn't have any idea how far away land was. He guessed it was 3,000 miles (4,800 km), but all he really knew was that he had to keep sailing west," said Mr. Rummage. "At times his crew got restless and complained, but they never came close to **mutiny** as some people say."

"I bet they thought they'd gone out for no good reason," said Hannah.

Mr. Rumage added "I'm sure they did, sometimes. But they were probably even more scared they'd never get home again."

"So how did Columbus manage to stay on track?" asked Hannah.

"Well, he had to rely on his experience, some guesswork, and plain luck!" laughed Mr. Rummage.

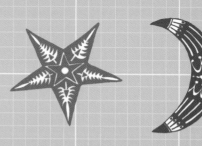

At the helm

Steering a ship and navigating the oceans was a tricky business in Columbus's time. It was very difficult to measure the distance a ship traveled because the instruments onboard weren't accurate. But Columbus was a genius at reading the signs of nature.

North, South, East, or West?

Occasionally, Columbus used a ship's compass. But after many days sailing west, his men were horrified to see that the needle was no longer pointing to the North Star as it normally did. Columbus calmed them down. Eventually he managed to explain that the North Star had moved slightly, not the needle. So they could still use the compass to navigate.

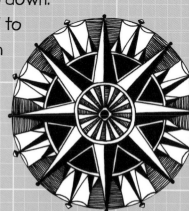

A MAGNETIC COMPASS WAS A MARINER'S MOST IMPORTANT INSTRUMENT OF NAVIGATION.

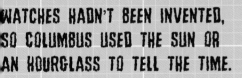

WATCHES HADN'T BEEN INVENTED, SO COLUMBUS USED THE SUN OR AN HOURGLASS TO TELL THE TIME.

Dead reckoning

Columbus probably relied on the simplest method of navigating, called dead reckoning. Each day he would measure the distance his ship had traveled and then mark its position on a chart. This would be the starting point for the next day's measurement, and so on.

COLUMBUS GOT HIS BEARINGS BY OBSERVING THE BEHAVIOR OF BIRDS IN THE SKY, HOW THE AIR SMELLED AND WHAT FLOATED PAST THE SHIP.

Columbus's logbooks

It's said that Columbus kept two logbooks to record how far he'd traveled: a true one for himself and a false one for his crew. He did this to comfort his crew so they wouldn't know how far away from home they were.

Strange sights

Columbus and his crew saw many strange sights along the way. At one point they crossed the Sargasso Sea—a huge mass of floating seaweed—and feared their ships might get tangled up in it and dragged to the bottom. But they soon forgot their fear, as they spotted the strange and beautiful fish that darted beneath the surface.

Land ahoy!

When Columbus and his men set foot on the tropical island he called San Salvador in 1492, he made history. Although he didn't know it, he had opened up a whole "New World" to Europeans.

The islanders

The first people he met were probably the Taino islanders. But because Columbus thought he had reached the Indies, he called them "Indians" and the name stuck. He thought that they were a fine-looking people who would make good "servants."

THE TAINOS WERE FRIENDLY AND WELCOMING.

A hero's welcome

Columbus sailed home in the Nina hoping to get to Spain before the Pinta. As it happened, Captain Pinzon and the Pinta actually reached Spain first, but only the northern tip. Columbus, however, landed in Portugal and was nearly prevented from getting home. But a hasty message to the Spanish monarchs helped and he reached home ahead of his rival. Columbus was welcomed as a hero and received his reward—although he'd turned up with just a few parrots, some sick "Indians," a pouch of gold, and some exotic plants.

COLUMBUS MAY WELL HAVE BROUGHT BACK PINEAPPLES AND MAIZE FROM THE WEST INDIES, AND POSSIBLY ALSO COCOA BEANS, PRICKLY PEARS, SQUASH, AND SWEET POTATOES.

"So who actually saw land first?" asked Digby.

Mr. Rummage gave him a conspiratorial look, "Well, it was the lookout, Rodriquez. He was the one who should have received the prize Queen Isabella had promised. But Christopher said that he'd seen a white streak on the horizon the night before, and claimed the reward for himself."

"What a sneak!" cried Hannah. "So he wasn't such a good captain after all. What happened then?"

"Columbus sailed around the coast and dropped anchor off an island he named San Salvador, which means "Holy Savior." Today, no one knows exactly which island it was, although it may have been Watling Island in the Bahamas."

"Was it a deserted island?" asked Digby excitedly.

"No, Columbus met some Native people there and traded with them before exploring more islands, including Cuba, which he thought was the mainland of Cathay, or modern China," Mr. Rummage went on. "But then, just before Christmas, the Santa Maria ran onto a coral reef and smashed."

"Oh no, what did he do?" asked Hannah.

"Luckily the islanders rushed to help them and most of their supplies were saved,"

Mr. Rummage went on. "Later, he used the wood from his ship to build a village, which he called La Navidad—Spanish for "Christmas" Then he set sail again, leaving 40 men behind to look for gold."

"Did they find any?" asked Digby.

"I'm afraid not. In the end, Columbus sailed home on the Nina. But he hadn't found all the treasure he'd been looking for, and arrived back at Palos with very little," said Mr. Rummage.

"What happened to the poor Taino people once they arrived in Spain?" asked Digby.

"Well," said Mr. Rummage, "Queen Isabella thought they should be sent home. She felt sorry for them. Actually, one of them was adopted by Columbus and later sailed with him on his other voyages."

"And the Tainos back in San Salvador?"

"Unfortunately, the Spanish didn't treat them well. Columbus thought they'd be good for manning Spanish ships—in fact, he thought of them as slaves. And because they weren't Christian, they were thought of as uncivilized. Europeans didn't think that they had a worthwhile culture of their own."

"That's terrible," said Hannah. "Why would anyone use human beings as slaves?"

"In those days, people thought that any discovered lands should belong, along with the people living on them, to the explorer's sponsors. In this case, it was the king and queen of Spain."

"But what if you just use religion as an excuse to steal from people or make them slaves? That can't be right," said Digby.

"Slavery is wrong," said Mr. Rummage. "But now I think we'd better go on with the story."

The Grand Fleet

Ferdinand and Isabella were spurred on by Columbus's promise of more gold and new land in the Indies. So they fitted out a Grand Fleet of 17 ships to make a second voyage in 1493. But this time, the ships contained 1,500 colonists. Spain was going to take over the new world Columbus had found.

La Navidad, Hispaniola

When the admiral fired a canon to signal his return to Hispaniola, there was no reply—no flag flying and no welcome. So Columbus went ashore, only to find that the settlement he had built, had been burned to the ground and the inhabitants massacred. No one knows exactly what happened, but it's likely that the Native people were so disgusted with the greed and brutality of the Spanish that they destroyed the settlement. From then on, Columbus's fortunes turned from bad to worse.

La Isabella

A short distance east of La Navidad, Columbus built the new settlement of Isabella, named after his queen. But it wasn't a good choice. The settlers weren't that interested in doing farm work. They wanted to find gold. So Columbus led an expedition inland to look for treasure. But when none was found, he began to capture and enslave Native people to work the land.

A TIGHTLY PACKED SLAVE SHIP

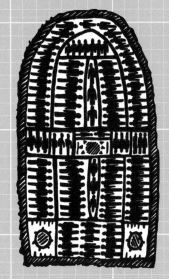

Settlers and Native People

The Native people grew more and more angry as the Spanish began raiding their villages, looking for riches. Some of the settlers complained of Columbus's cruelty and greed. Others became sick and died, or went home. Columbus finally left his brother in charge of the colony and returned to Spain, a bitter and disappointed man.

A new continent

As Columbus sailed along the coast of South America, he came across a huge outflow of water. It was the mouth of the Orinoco river, leading from the Atlantic Ocean to Venezuela. He knew then that what he had found must be a very large mass of land. He reported back to Spain that he had found another world. He called it the "Garden of Eden."

Trinidad and Jamaica

Columbus went on to discover more islands. He named one of them Trinidad, after the Holy Trinity, and the other Jamaica, similar to the Taino word, Xamacca.

Columbus in disgrace

When Columbus arrived back in Spain, he was brought before the king and queen. Isabella forgave Columbus for his mistakes in Hispaniola, but she wouldn't give him back his titles. Columbus spent the next two years in deep despair.

THE TAINOS SLEPT ON WOVEN HAMMOCKS. COLUMBUS BROUGHT ONE HOME WITH HIM. IT'S BEEN THE TRADITIONAL SAILOR'S BED EVER SINCE.

"So, although Columbus and the Spanish king and queen had high hopes for the second voyage," said Mr. Rummage, "it was a disaster. And he'd lost the friendship of the Native people by treating them so badly."

"I bet he was in trouble when he got back," said Hannah.

"Not exactly. He managed to return before bad reports of him reached home. But another year went by before he was given provisions for a third voyage."

"He just wouldn't give up, would he?" said Digby admiringly.

"No, he was determined to get to Cathay or Cipango. And he wanted to keep an eye on the settlers he'd left behind. He thought they were lazy and couldn't be trusted."

"So the third voyage was doomed from the start," muttered Hannah.

"You could say that," replied Mr. Rummage. "He set off with six ships but was held up for weeks in the doldrums— an area of calm water near the Equator, with no sea current or winds. When he finally moved out of it, Columbus found an island he called Trinidad, and another one, which he called Jamaica."

"But what about Hispaniola and the settlers?" asked Digby.

"When Columbus finally arrived in Hispaniola, he found a land at war. One group of settlers backed Columbus's brother, who governed the island, while another backed a rebel called Francisco Roldan. It took two years to end the rebellion."

"Couldn't Ferdinand and Isabella have helped?" asked Hannah.

"Well, they sent a judge to settle things, but he put Columbus and his family in chains for being hard and greedy governors. They were stripped of their honors and shipped home in disgrace."

"**W**asn't it about time Columbus gave up his wandering and settled down?" asked Hannah. "After all, he was probably getting old."

"You'd think so," said Mr. Rummage, "but that wasn't his way. He suggested yet another voyage, and the Spanish monarchs were happy to see him go."

"Not very surprising if he was still pestering them about the Indies!" laughed Digby.

"Exactly," smiled Mr. Rummage. "Although a Portuguese explorer called Da Gama had just found a way around Africa to India. So Ferdinand and Isabella were probably willing to give Columbus one more chance to find an even better way. But they made it clear he was to look for gold, silver, and spices—and not go anywhere near Hispaniola!"

"I bet he didn't pay any attention to them" said Hannah.

"You're right," said Mr. Rummage. "But it wasn't his fault. He was forced to anchor off Hispaniola in June of 1502, because he was afraid a hurricane was coming."

"Did the new governor let him in?" asked Digby.

"No, and the hurricane came. Columbus hid in a small bay close by and saved his ships. But the rest of the trip was a disaster. He lost his fleet and returned to Spain in 1504, as a passenger in a borrowed ship!"

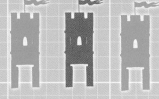

The high voyage

When Columbus arrived at the port in Hispaniola on his fourth voyage, Governor Ovando refused to let him in. Christopher explained that a hurricane was brewing and his ships needed shelter. The governor ignored him. But nature was on Columbus's side. While he took cover in a nearby bay, Ovando lost 24 ships when the hurricane struck. The dead included Columbus's enemies, the judge Bobadilla, and the rebel Roldan. Christopher must have thought they'd got what they deserve, especially since the ship carrying his own share of the colony's wealth made it all the way back to Spain!

COLUMBUS FIGHTS THE NATIVE AMERICANS AT RIO BELEN.

Rio Belen

Columbus went to the mouth of the Rio Belen in western Panama. He set up a fort, or a base from which to explore inland. But a group of Native people attacked the fort and Columbus was forced to abandon one of his ships to make a quick getaway with the remaining three.

Panama Straits

Leaving Hispaniola behind, Columbus sailed into the Panama Straits. Here, he heard tales of a huge stretch of water that lay just a few days march from the coast. But he was in too much of a hurry to investigate. Had he done so, he might have been the first European to see the Pacific Ocean from the shores of the New World.

Homeward bound

Marooned

Columbus's ships were rotten and began to leak badly. Sea worms had eaten into the wood. Eventually they were beached and abandoned off the coast of Jamaica, leaving Columbus and 100 men **marooned** for over a year.

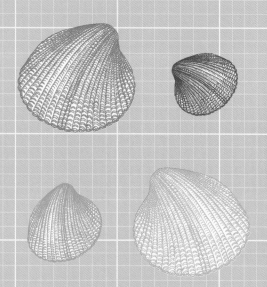

Malaria and mutiny

As time went on, many sailors, including Columbus, fell ill with malaria and other tropical diseases. When he tried to create order and discipline, half of them mutinied.

Columbus tricks the Jamaicans

The Jamaicans, who had provided Columbus and his crew with food and supplies, suddenly refused to bring any more. The men became sick and weak. But Columbus tricked the Jamaicans by saying he would block out the sun from the sky if they didn't bring food. In reality, he knew an eclipse of the sun was coming. The islanders were frightened by Columbus's "powers" and soon began helping out again.

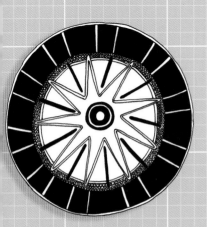

A SUNBIRD AND SUN WHEEL, INSPIRED BY SOLAR ECLIPSES. THE BIRD HAS A SUN-LIKE EYE IN THE CENTER OF ITS BODY.

Rescued at last!

Finally, a brave sailor named Diego Salcedo agreed to paddle a canoe across the channel to Hispaniola to get help. On arrival, he asked Ovando for a ship, but the governor made him wait seven months before providing one. Columbus returned to Spain, brokenhearted.

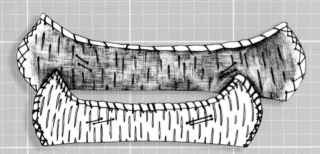

"He was one lucky explorer," said Digby. "Look at the number of times he could have been killed."

"Yes," agreed Hannah, "and not just by hostile Native people—by his own men as well. He could have drowned, or died of disease."

"Unfortunately it was the Tainos who died of diseases brought over by the settlers on Columbus's voyages," said Mr. Rummage. "Apparently there were over a million people living in the islands before Columbus came. But twenty years later, over half had died."

"Oh no!" said Digby. "That's what sickness can do?"

"Yes, and slavery and fighting" replied Mr. Rummage. "Still, today we usually celebrate Columbus for the positive things he did—his discoveries."

"So how is Columbus celebrated, Mr. Rummage?" asked Hannah.

"Well, there's Columbus Day and many places are named after him, such as British Columbia in Canada and Columbus, Ohio, in the United States."

"But why weren't the Americas named after Columbus?" asked Digby.

"Because they were named after the explorer Amerigo Vespucci," said Mr. Rummage. "But that's another story."

"So what happened to Christopher?" asked Digby. "I mean, he did so much and yet it seems like no one wanted to have anything to do with him at the end."

"It wasn't quite like that," said Mr. Rummage. "Although there are stories that he was left on his own to die in poverty."

"Couldn't Queen Isabella help him?" asked Hannah. "She seemed to like him."

"Unfortunately the queen was very sick. She died not long after Columbus returned. And Columbus wasn't well either. His years at sea, bad food, and rheumatism finally caught up with him."

"He must have been disappointed," said Digby. "After all, he never did find a route to Asia."

"He never stopped believing he had found Asia, though. He spent months resting in a monastery. Then he began writing letters to the king to get his titles back. He didn't get them, but he did get a percentage of the riches of the Indies."

"Plenty of gold?" asked Digby.

"Well, he was able to live comfortably enough, although he still died a sad man..."

"Hey, Mrs. Bilge, what are you doing?" cried Digby as the market cleaner shoved a yellowed piece of parchment into her cart."

"Always garbage lying around," grumbled Mrs. Bilge. "Why can't you keep the place tidy?"

Hannah jumped to the rescue and pulled the map from Mrs. Bilge's cart.

"That's still not garbage Mrs. Bilge. It's a valuable map."

Mrs. Bilge replied "Looks like garbage to me."

"I'm going to see Mr. Clumpmugger right now to see if he'll put it in a frame to keep it safe," said Digby. "Then I'll hang it on the wall above all my other treasures. It deserves that."

"Right!," said Mr. Rummage with a twinkle in his eye. "Goodbye then both of you, and see you next Saturday."

 # The Americas

The land that Columbus came upon was finally named after Amerigo Vespucci, a sailor who journeyed to the Indies in 1501. Vespucci claimed he had found new land. So the Americas were named after him. It was only later that people realized Columbus had discovered it earlier.

Columbus Day

In the United States, the second Monday of October is a holiday called Columbus Day, in memory of Christopher Columbus. Some people call it Discovery Day, or Landing Day. In some of the biggest American cities such as New York, Los Angeles, and San Francisco, special parades are held on this day. In Spain and South America, Columbus Day is celebrated on October 12 each year.

ALMOST EVERY CITY IN THE UNITED STATES HAS A STATUE OF CHRISTOPHER COLUMBUS.

The truth and the legend

Much of what we know about Columbus's first voyage comes from the log he wrote during the trip. But it's not the original log. All we have is a copy made by a man called La Cassa. Part of it is written as if Columbus himself was talking, the rest is a narrative of events. But because the document isn't original, we need to be careful about the facts.

Some parts might be exaggerations to make his voyages sound more exciting. Other people have written about Columbus, but after his death. His son is one of them, but we can't be sure that everything he wrote actually happened. What we do know, however, is that a lot of myths and legends have sprung up around Columbus's discoveries.

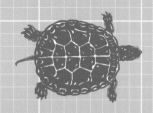

HERE ARE SOME OF THE FACTS AND THE FICTION OF COLUMBUS'S AMAZING STORY:

FICTION: Columbus set out to prove the Earth was round.
FACT: In 1492 most people knew that it was, although they didn't know its size.

FICTION: Queen Isabella sold her crown jewels to finance Columbus's first voyage.
FACT: The town of Palos supplied two of the ships, and Italian financing helped. Little came from the Spanish treasury.

FICTION: Columbus's crew were nothing but a bunch of criminals.
FACT: The crew were experienced sailors. A royal pardon was offered to criminals who wanted to enlist, but just four took up the offer.

FICTION: The initial voyage was difficult.
FACT: There were no storms and no one died.

FICTION: Columbus commanded a large fleet and a huge crew on his first voyage.
FACT: Just 90 men sailed three tiny (by modern standards) ships.

FICTION: Columbus died poor and in prison.
FACT: He was relatively well off and died with his family around him.

FICTION: Columbus was the first European to set foot on North American soil.
FACT: He sailed around the Caribbean islands and along the coasts of Central and South America.

Glossary

astronomy The scientific study of stars and other bodies in outer space

bow The front part of a ship or boat

coffer A place where money is kept

expedition A journey made by a group of people that has a definite purpose

Genoese The people of Genoa, a city in northwest Italy

geometry The mathematics of the measurement and relationships of points, lines, angles, surfaces, and solids

mariner A person who navigates or assists in navigating a ship

maroon To abandon someone without intending to rescue them

mutiny A rebellion of sailors against their superior officers

rigging The ropes and chains used to support and control the masts and sails of a sailing ship

shipwreck Destruction of a ship by storm or collision

stern The rear part of a ship or boat

Index

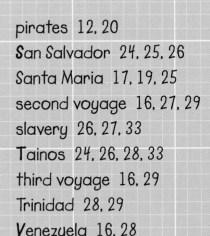

chart 8, 9, 12, 17, 23
coat of arms 9, 15
continents 11, 17, 28
crew 18, 21, 22, 32, 36
Dona Felipe 12
first voyage 6, 17, 36
fourth voyage 16, 31
Hispaniola 16, 27, 28, 29, 30, 31, 33

Jamaica 16, 28, 29, 32
King Ferdinand and Queen Isabella 14, 15, 17, 18, 25, 26, 27, 28, 29, 30, 34, 36
King John of Portugal 13
navigating 22, 23
Nina 17, 19, 24, 25
Panama 16, 31
Pinta 17, 19, 24

pirates 12, 20
San Salvador 24, 25, 26
Santa Maria 17, 19, 25
second voyage 16, 27, 29
slavery 26, 27, 33
Tainos 24, 26, 28, 33
third voyage 16, 29
Trinidad 28, 29
Venezuela 16, 28

Other characters in the Stories of Great People series.

KENZO the barber has a wig or hairpiece for every occasion, and is always happy to put his scissors to use!

CHRISSY's vintage clothing stall has all the costumes Digby and Hannah need to act out the characters in Mr. Rummage's stories.

YOUSSEF has traveled to many places around the world. He carries a bag full of souvenirs from his exciting journeys.

SAFFRON sells pots and pans, herbs, spices, oils, soaps, and dyes from her spice kitchen stall.

BUZZ is a street vendor with all the gossip. He sells treats from a tray that's strapped around his neck.

Mr. POLLOCK's toy stall is filled with string puppets, rocking horses, model planes, wooden animals—and he makes them all himself!

PIXIE the market's fortuneteller sells incense, lotions and potions, candles, mandalas, and crystals inside her exotic stall.

PRU is a dreamer and Hannah's best friend. She likes to visit the market with Digby and Hannah, especially when makeup and dressing up is involved.

JAKE is Digby's friend. He's got a lively imagination and is always up to mischief.

COLONEL KARBUNCLE sells military uniforms, medals, flags, swords, helmets, cannon balls—all from the trunk of his old jeep.